GW00862889

MOTIVATION

MOTIVATION

by William A. Simpson

The Industrial Society

First published 1983 by
The Industrial Society
Robert Hyde House
48 Bryanston Square
London W1H 7LN
Telephone 071-262 2401

Second edition 1989
© *The Industrial Society, 1983, 1989*
Reprinted November 1990

ISBN 0 85290 414 2

British Library Cataloguing in Publication Data:
Simpson, William A.
    Motivation – 2nd ed.
    1. Job enrichment
    I. Title   II. Industrial Society   III. Series
    658.3'1423

Typeset by Columns of Reading
Printed and bound in Great Britain by Belmont Press, Northampton

CONTENTS

FOREWORD

Whatever the discipline or level of management, the responsibilities of a manager are many and various. It is their job to produce results with essentially just two resources—people and time.

To maximise the potential of both, most managers need some reminders and basic guidelines to help them.

The Notes for Managers series provides succinct yet comprehensive coverage of key management issues and skills. The short time it takes to read each title will pay dividends in terms of utilising one of those key resources—people.

A crucial factor in achieving success in industry and commerce is the ability to motivate all of the people involved in the operation. This short book sets out in very practical terms what needs to be done by managers if people are to be motivated, and if they are to achieve their potential. It will be useful for those who buy it individually, but organisations will benefit by ensuring that all their staff in charge of others have a copy.

ALISTAIR GRAHAM
Director, The Industrial Society

I

INTRODUCTION

1

MOTIVATION

What is motivation?

Motivation is what makes people do things. In another sense it is what makes them put real effort and energy into what they do. Obviously it varies in nature and intensity from individual to individual, depending on the particular mixture of influences at any given moment.

In short, a simple definition of motivation could be:

'Getting people to do willingly and well those things which have to be done.'

It has been stated that:

- positive motivation occurs when people 'give' to a request
- motivation ceases when people are 'compelled' to surrender to a demand.

The importance of motivation

Motivation is vital in any job if people are to give their best to it. Assuming that employees are given opportunity for good performance and have the necessary skills, then effectiveness depends on their motivation. People are undoubtedly a most critical resource and no matter what the degree of sophistication we rise to in our technology, we will still depend on the 'human factor'.

Who is responsible?

It is the job of work-group leaders or team leaders to motivate their teams. It is they who are best placed to create the correct environment in which people will 'grow' and give of their best to their work. It has to be recognised that certain factors are often outside their span of control or influence, e.g. pay, status, terms and conditions of employment. However, practical experience has shown that these people can provide recognition, responsibility, and work which is challenging—all of these having proved to be among the greatest motivating factors.

Signs of motivation

The attitudes and behaviour of employees very often reflect motivation or the lack of it.

Examples of the signs of motivation are:

- high performance and results being consistently achieved
- the energy, enthusiasm, and determination to succeed
- unstinting co-operation in overcoming problems
- the willingness of individuals to accept responsibility
- willingness to accommodate necessary change.

Lack of motivation

Conversely, employees who are de-motivated or who lack motivation often display:

- apathy and indifference to the job
- a poor record of time-keeping and high absenteeism
- an exaggeration of the effects/difficulties encountered in problems, disputes and grievances
- a lack of co-operation in dealing with problems or difficulties
- unjustified resistance to change.

Managers generally deplore employees' lack of motivation and interest in the company and in their work. Many men and women turn their excess energies and talents to hobbies and merely tolerate their jobs as a way of earning their living so they can afford to meet the challenge of life in leisure-time activities. It is not leisure as a pursuit, but work as a drudgery, that is to be condemned.

So many repetitive, monotonous, and uninteresting jobs could be made more palatable if managers recognised the rights of individuals. Countless people have the elements of challenge and interest in them destroyed by managers' failure to recognise human needs and motivations.

2

THE BEHAVIOURAL
SCIENTISTS

Over the years a growing number of behavioural scientists have carried out their own investigations into what makes people 'tick'. It would be wrong to ignore this accumulated knowledge, but equally wrong to pretend that each viewpoint in itself holds the key to solving our problems of motivating people. The results and findings of some, however, do give an insight of practical significance which can be helpful to the understanding of the line manager.

A.H. Maslow

Maslow's thinking is centred on a hierarchy of the individual's needs and is outlined as follows.

The needs hierarchy

1 Based on needs not wants.
2 Operates on an ascending scale. As one need becomes fulfilled the next ascendant need is uncovered.
3 We can 'revert back', i.e. people operating at level 4 or 5 will revert to level 2 if a feeling of insecurity takes over. Once this need is met, however, they will return to their former needs area.
4 Needs not being met are demonstrated in behaviour, and managers must create an 'environment' in which motivation can take place.
5 To avoid apathy, which finally results when needs are

unfulfilled, managers must be able to implement the right action at the right time.

Put another way, Maslow is asking the questions:

- Where do you think you really are?
- Where are you going?

Individual needs

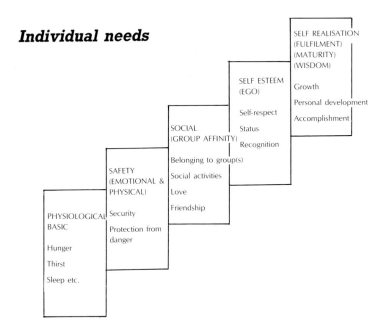

SELF REALISATION
(FULFILMENT)
(MATURITY)
(WISDOM)

Growth

Personal development

Accomplishment

SELF ESTEEM
(EGO)

Self-respect

Status

Recognition

SOCIAL
(GROUP AFFINITY)

Belonging to group(s)

Social activities

Love

Friendship

SAFETY
(EMOTIONAL &
PHYSICAL)

Security

Protection from
danger

PHYSIOLOGICAL
BASIC

Hunger

Thirst

Sleep etc.

D. McGregor

Douglas McGregor (quoting A.H. Maslow) suggests that people's needs can be depicted in a kind of hierarchy. At the bottom of the triangle are the needs of our animal nature for self-preservation—for sleep, for food and water, for shelter and warmth. These needs are basic; as someone aptly said: 'Man does not live by bread alone, except when there is no bread.' Once satisfied, they cease to be strong motivators to action. Thus, as western societies begin to feel more materially secure, their higher needs for self-expression (including the drive for achievement), for an objective, for self-fulfilment, clamour for satisfaction. It follows, therefore, that in suitable circumstances and with proper management, the majority of people can be self-directed if they become committed to an objective they value. They will not only accept responsibility but often will seek it. Further, to work is as natural as to eat or to sleep. Creativity is widely, not narrowly, scattered among the population. (This is McGregor's 'Theory Y'.)

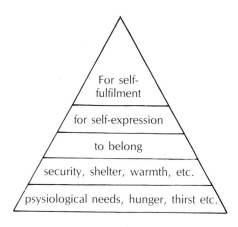

In short, people can be self-motivated. The task of the manager is to create conditions of work in which, and through which, self-motivation can find its release. In situations where this is difficult to achieve—as in dull, repetitive work—higher pay remains of paramount importance, since workers are forced to find satisfaction outside the work situation.

If Theory X is to be our assumption and we treat people accordingly we find out nothing about them and our beliefs will become a self-fulfilling prophesy, i.e. people will need close supervision, firm discipline, incentive schemes, etc.

If, however, we believe that Theory Y is correct and treat people accordingly, we shall find out what they are really like. The answer will be that they are all different and we can then manage them according to their strengths and weaknesses.

Table 1. Attitudes to work (the X–Y theory)

Theory X	Theory Y
1 People dislike work and will avoid it if possible	**1** Work is necessary to people's psychological growth
2 People must be forced or bribed to make the right effort	**2** People want to be interested in their work and, under the right conditions, they can enjoy it
3 People would rather be directed than accept responsibilities, which they avoid	**3** People will direct themselves towards an accepted target
	4 People will seek, and accept, responsibility under the right conditions
	5 The discipline people impose on themselves is more effective, and can be more severe, than any imposed on them
4 People are motivated mainly by money	**6** Under the right conditions, people are motivated by the desire to realise their own potential
5 People are motivated by anxiety about their security	**7** Creativity and ingenuity are widely distributed and grossly under-used
6 Most people have little creativity—except when getting round management rules!	

The key is in not making assumptions but in giving opportunity for achievement, responsibility, creativity and in utilising talent, abilities, interests, etc. in so far as the task allows (see Table 1).

F. Herzberg

Frederick Herzberg asked many people in different jobs at different levels, two questions.

- What factors lead you to experience extreme dissatisfaction with your job?
- What factors lead you to experience extreme satisfaction with your job?

He collated the answers and displayed them in the form of a chart which shows the order and frequency in which the factors appeared (see Fig. 3).

Dissatisfaction

Factors on the left of the chart show a greater potential for dissatisfaction than satisfaction. Improving them or giving people more of them:

1 does not create a motivational atmosphere
2 creates only short-lived satisfaction, because they become accepted as the norm.

In Herzberg's words: 'You just remove unhappiness, you don't make people happy.'
These factors match levels 1, 2 and 3 of the Maslow hierarchy and are connected with the job context. Herzberg called them the 'hygiene factors'.

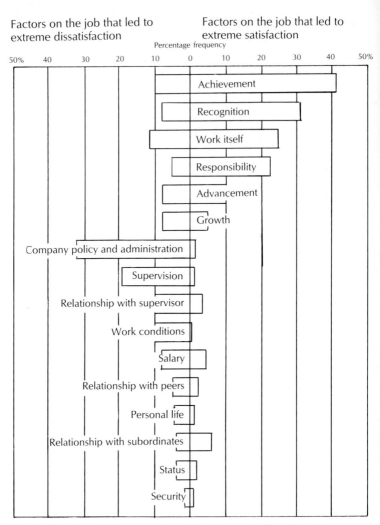

Factors on the job that led to extreme dissatisfaction

Factors on the job that led to extreme satisfaction

Percentage frequency

50% 40 30 20 10 0 10 20 30 40 50%

Achievement

Recognition

Work itself

Responsibility

Advancement

Growth

Company policy and administration

Supervision

Relationship with supervisor

Work conditions

Salary

Relationship with peers

Personal life

Relationship with subordinates

Status

Security

Fig. 3. Herzberg's factors of satisfaction and dissatisfaction

Satisfaction

Factors on the right of the chart have little to do with money and status; much to do with achievement and responsibility. They match levels 4 and 5 of the Maslow hierarchy and are connected with the job content. Herzberg called them the 'motivators'.

The work itself

The chart shows that the nature of the work itself has potential for both satisfaction and dissatisfaction. The moral for managers is clear—they should pay particular attention to the kind of tasks they expect people to do. Where these are boring and repetitive they should strive to create a motivational atmosphere by paying special attention to other factors.

The Hawthorne experiments

Management has been unwilling to recognise the impact of motivation on the conduct of employees and hence on the productivity of the enterprise. Although the most significant findings on this subject became known more than 40 years ago and sounded the death knell on the totally mechanistic approach of scientific management, many thousands of practising managers have failed to pay heed to these

Changes in working conditions	Results
Day work to piece work	Increased output
Five minute rest periods morning and afternoon	Increased output
Rest period increased to 10 minutes	Greater increased output
Six 5-minute rest periods	Output fell: workers explained that their work rhythm was interrupted
Return to two rest periods, the first with a free hot meal	Increased output
Girls permitted to go home at 4.30 p.m. instead of 5.00 p.m.	Increased output
All improvements in working conditions rescinded. Girls returned to 48-hour week, with no rest periods, no piece work, and no free meals	Output increased to highest point recorded during entire period

findings. In its attempt to eliminate variables and predict results, management has tried to depersonalise the organisation. Scientific management, with its accent on efficiency, believes people are motivated only by material considerations and, therefore, their actions can be ordered without regard to personal attitudes and behaviour.

The shortcomings of these beliefs were first brought to light in what later became known as the Hawthorne experiments which were conducted between 1924 and 1927 at the Hawthorne Works of the Western Electric Company in Chicago. The management wished to increase the productivity of its workers and experimented with working conditions.

While productivity went up and later settled at a lower level, which was still higher than the initial level, the conclusions that were drawn were:

- that improvements in working conditions in themselves will provide only a short-term stimulus to higher performance
- that, in the long run, continued improvement is dependent on other factors, for example the extent to which people are allowed to grow within the job.

II

MOTIVATION IN PRACTICE

1

PRACTICAL ACTIONS

Practical steps in motivation

It has been said that there are four kinds of people in the world:

- people who watch things happen
- people to whom things happen
- people who do not know what is happening
- people who make things happen.

If managers are to be the ones who make things happen through other people, they must be aware of how they can get people to work willingly and well, to increase people's satisfaction in their job, and the organisation's efficiency.

Every manager must then *make subordinates feel valued* by:

- regularly monitoring the subordinate's work
- sharing an interest in subordinates' lives and in whatever they hold important
- creating an atmosphere of approval and co-operation
- ensuring every subordinate understands the importance of his or her contribution to the team's/department's/organisation's objectives
- ensuring every subordinate understands the function and philosophy of the organisation and why work matters.

Provide opportunities for development by:

- setting standards and targets for all subordinates
- providing on and off the job training

- arranging any necessary internal and external contacts
- using subordinates to train others in the specialist skills they may have
- structuring or grouping tasks to use the subordinates' skills/gifts to the fullest.

Recognise achievements by:

- praising and communicating individual successes
- reporting regularly on the team's progress
- holding regular meetings to monitor and counsel on an individual's progress towards targets
- explaining the organisation's results and achievements.

Provide a challenge by:

- setting and communicating the team's/department's/ organisation's objectives
- providing scope for individuals to take greater responsibility
- encouraging ideas and where practical by allowing subordinates the responsibility for implementing them.

2

MOTIVATING CHANGE

Change is normal. Change is an inherent part of life. Why then do all people, managers and workers alike, constantly resist it?

Sir Barnes Wallis was once quoted as saying: 'We are all suspicious of other people's ideas.'

Can resistance to change be regarded as abnormal or pathological? One point of view holds that it is more a 'symptom' than a disease.

When resistance does appear it should not be thought of

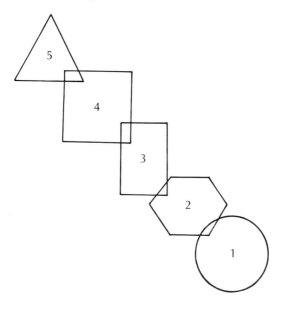

Fig. 4. Symbolic illustration of stages during a process of change.

as something to be overcome. Instead it can best be thought of as a useful red flag—a signal that something is wrong. Undoubtedly one of the most challenging roles which a manager plays is that of *motivating change*.

Implementing change is about starting, changing gear, stopping, accelerating, slowing down and arriving. The theme throughout is about involving others and being co-operative, willing, and flexible. While we may not waver from our final objective, our activities and circumstances may change in the process of reaching that goal.

Symbolically we intend to make a triangle—circumstances demand a circle. Only with flexibility can we effect change (*see* Fig. 4). Motivating and managing change requires:

- the full co-operation of all concerned in the business
- an effective method of communication which is two-way at all stages and levels
- effective feedback to the decision-making centre of progress and obstacles.

Change has very often to be effected while maintaining present procedures and, if this is to be achieved, it requires the *full co-operation* of the participants, e.g. subordinates, managers, all employees below first-line supervision, customers, suppliers, and trade unions.

Gaining *willing consent* throughout the course of effecting change is positive motivation.

3

INTRODUCING CHANGES

Examples of change

1 Major changes:
- altering pay or bonus systems
- introducing new equipment or machinery
- making a major change in procedure
- introducing work measurement

2 Minor changes:
- moving a subordinate from one job to another
- making a small alteration in work method
- modifying the time of tea or lunch breaks
- altering canteen prices

Change is inevitable and is a continuing process. Even minor changes may have major repercussions; for what appears to be a minor change to the manager may seem a major one to the employees affected.

Why do people resist change?

They resist not because of the change itself, but because it means adjusting themselves to a changed situation, and because of fears such as:

- loss of job
- loss of skills
- inability to cope with change
- loss of earnings
- loss of status

- loss of companions (owing to work reorganisation)
- loss of familiar surroundings.

How should managers introduce change?

'Communication and consultation are particularly important in times of change. The achievement of change is a joint concern of management and employees, and should be carried out in a way which pays regard both to the efficiency of the undertaking and to the interests of employees. Major changes in working agreements should not be made by management without prior discussion with employees or their representatives.'

(*Industrial Relations Code of Practice*)

1 *Plan:* taking into account who it will affect and how it will affect them.
2 *Explain:* the need for change—by managers briefing down the line to all those affected.
3 *Consult those affected or their representatives:*
  - it tells them that their views are being considered, resulting in increased willingness to co-operate
  - it tells you of their specific anxieties, allowing you to take these problems into account
  - consultation may bring out important factors previously overlooked.

Analyse

Consider and act on the results of consultation. In particular:

- reconsider your original plan
- arrange for demonstration of any new equipment
- give reassurance of no redundancy or loss of earnings (when possible)
- take steps to provide training.

Communicate and implement the change

The reasons for change and its impact on those affected, must be communicated by managers briefing down the line to all employees concerned, supporting this with adequate written information and/or instructions.

Follow up

Ensure that the change has proceeded as planned, and that the objective has been achieved. Further consultation, readjustment and communication may be necessary.

4

MOTIVATION AT DIFFERENT LEVELS

The actions of motivating can vary depending on where you are operating within an organisation. In order to highlight this, three managers at different levels have expressed what they consider are the practical actions paramount to ensuring the highest degree of motivation in their subordinate staff.

At the top
Sir Peter White

At the top you will be dealing with people—senior people—and (if the top is high enough) not much else. So people issues will fill your day and success or failure will be in your leadership area.

How will you motivate your senior managers? Remember that at that stage both you and they:

- will have known for years about Herzberg, Drucker, Maslow, and the more reputable parts of the behavioural sciences
- will have reached the present positions by achieving tasks, building teams, developing individuals, and concentrating on what a leader does
- will have developed your qualities to the point where they are not going to change much—if at all.

So how do you motivate your senior managers?
This is the level at which 'inspirational' as opposed to

'mechanical' leadership has a very definite part to play. Whether you are successful in that, and thus in motivating your senior managers, will depend very largely upon how you have prepared yourself for the top position and the attributes you have acquired in the process.

Specifically it will depend on your ability to:

- take responsibility and not duck it
- promote confidence by acting, and looking the part
- project a cheerful, hopeful, enthusiastic, encouraging, and optimistic image
- avoid fussing, worrying, and constant interference
- walk the job and be seen
- set the right example in your personal life, off the job
- think positively
- be one of the 'new ideas' people in your organisation
- be seen to be an opportunist
- accept and capitalise on change
- learn new tricks as they come along
- show that you care for those under you
- have the moral courage to take the right—albeit the unpopular—decision
- match your dedication to the organisation by equal dedication to the one above (if there is one)
- have the courage to delegate
- take hard decisions, remove 'passengers' and dead wood
- communicate continuously to all points of the compass
- listen
- avoid needless confrontations
- recognise and deal with stress in yourself and others
- pick winners
- enthuse people—what is now called 'charisma'
- make people laugh (but only if you can do it naturally).

So what is the proof that you are motivating your senior managers successfully? Well, it has been said a million times and it was said again after the Falklands affair by the senior 'managers' of HMS Invincible about their Captain: 'I would follow that man anywhere and do anything for him.'

In the middle

Reg Blundell

For seven hectic years I was General Manager of British Telecom, based in Aberdeen, which supplies and maintains telecommunications for a quarter of a million customers in the North of Scotland.

The boom brought by North Sea oil stimulated a doubling of our system size in just over five years, a record unparalleled in British telecommunications history. We urgently built many new telephone exchanges and radio stations, expanded our trunk and local networks spread over 14,000 square miles, and extended our engineering bases to accommodate over 1000 vehicles and nearly as many mechanical aids.

Numerous managers and skilled workers left us for employment in North Sea industries, which drained the local labour markets. Nevertheless, we built up a tip-top team of over 3000 personnel, whose achievements are a remarkable success story. We have greatly improved the quality of customer service, markedly reduced costs, increased productivity, and improved customer and indus-trial relations.

Obviously the credit goes to the staff at large and reflects grinding hard work done at all levels, including the Board of Management of which I was Chairman—but the make or break point in the management chain was at middle management level.

While building up our labour force and our management team we had invaluable help from The Industrial Society. The investment has paid off profitably.

The role of the senior manager is to guide middle managers in translating business policies and directives into acceptable and feasible work commitments, objectives, and targets.

The senior manager should clarify the following with middle managers—their:

- duties and responsibilities

- objectives and targets
- performance levels, i.e. standards of quality, quantity, cost, and completion dates
- resource levels—manpower, machines, and money
- levels of authority and accountability
- relationships with other middle managers' working groups
- scope of personal action, and when to call for help.

Middle managers should have professional expertise and a sound technical knowledge of the work, gained as a first-line manager, but their wider span of control requires enhanced training in the following:

- leading professional teams
- industrial relations and negotiation
- management of people and motivation
- Action-Centred Leadership
- creative thinking and problem solving
- communication (team briefing groups)

(It is in the foregoing that we have had help from The Industrial Society.)

The middle manager will repeat the senior manager's actions with individual first-line managers by agreeing their objectives and targets—and preparing back-up action plans and work programmes.

The senior manager will:

- leave the middle manager the maximum scope for getting on with the work unhindered but will be readily available for consultation and guidance
- deter newly appointed middle managers from a natural tendency to bypass their first-line managers
- encourage the middle manager to delegate and devolve to the full, learning when to check and when to trust
- equip the middle manager with efficient means of monitoring work flow which detect early signs of developing trouble which can be nipped in the bud, i.e. 'exception reporting'

- encourage middle managers to be decisive, developing their own management style
- discourage 'perfectionism' which escalates costs and stresses subordinates
- encourage the production of commercially acceptable standards which create customer and worker satisfaction
- only judge mistakes after all the facts are established, giving constructive criticism and remedial guidance in *strict privacy*
- after judgement, consider mistakes as closed chapters, except for avoiding repetitions
- do a periodic review with each middle manager making a 'stock take' of:

  i the adequacy of their resources
  ii the progress of their action plans and programmes, with estimated out-turns compared with targets
  iii any likely shortfalls and their causes
  iv major problems (devise remedial measures)
  v what help if any is required from senior managers

- let middle managers know exactly how they stand, i.e. how their own efforts and those of their group are assessed and valued
- teach the principles of creative thinking and problem-solving and demonstrate by personal example
- inculcate the philosophy that the essence of the middle manager's job is finding problems and solving them much earlier than the problem can find the middle manager
- give credit publicly when credit is due.

Over the years I have quizzed many people at all levels on what qualities they most admired in the best managers for whom they had worked. The mixture is nearly the same as before:

- they really know the job and do it well
- they never panic
- they tell you exactly what they expect

- you know precisely how you stand with them
- they are fair and have neither favourites nor scapegoats
- you felt you could never let them down
- I really enjoyed working for them.

If you are a senior manager, stare into this mirror of personal needs, and ask yourself if you see your own reflection. If you do you may take modest pride that you have the rare qualities which make people want to work well and willingly for you.

At the front line
Allison Grant

Working in the catering trade, especially being involved with exhibition work, some of the main responsibilities lie with the setting up and running of different types of restaurants and catering outlets.

All staff I engage often work only for the period of one show: this can be a greater advantage than it is a disadvantage.

'Motivation at the front line'—quite a difficult subject to write about, so the first thing I thought about was to see the immediate reaction from a group of boys working under pressure in a wash-up area, in a real situation.

We walked into the hot, steamy area and pointed to the title—the immediate chorus that followed was:

'But we are playing a very important role, this is a vital job, you need us.'

To me, motivating at the front line, e.g. porters and washing-up staff, can be aided if they are treated as people: even though it is an incredibly rotten job, it is essential that they realise just how important their role is in the operation as a whole, and for the supervisor to gain their respect.

I always try to create a good working atmosphere, and get the wash-up area working as a team—the hardest thing to do is to weed out the odd ones who are not pulling their weight. If all the boys are working together and hard, it does a great deal to motivate them.

Often wash-up areas do not operate as a team, but just an individual washing pots all day—motivation here is even harder.

The person working here might not be the brightest or quickest of staff, but is doing a worthwhile job, and you have really got to be genuinely polite and respect that person's intelligence. To give the person pride in the job, provide a smart respectable uniform so that the person feels involved and part of the operation and of course 'praise' the individual—which is often forgotten because the person is behind the scenes.

With my staff, many of whom work only for one show, I always try and get some kind of feedback to my methods or systems; should I abolish them, or improve them? Hopefully I try and make the next porter's life that little bit easier or more enjoyable!

To me, showing concern and interest in their problems and difficulties, but still being firm and putting them under pressures, e.g. deadlines and time limits, can be an extremely effective motivator.

Sir Peter White was an Associate Director at The Industrial Society. He served for 40 years in The Royal Navy where he rose to the rank of admiral. Sir Peter was responsible for 63,000 civilians in naval dockyards.

Reg Blundell is a former General Manager of British Telecom, Aberdeen and North of Scotland area. He was responsible for 3210 employees.

Allison Grant is a catering supervisor with John Sutcliffe and Co Ltd.

5

A FINAL WORD

Motivational skills can be developed but their development requires concentration, effort, and practice. It is necessary for the motivator (the leader) to translate his or her basic knowledge of human behaviour into day-to-day leadership action which will in turn bring about the required results and the accomplishment of the task.

III

APPENDICES

APPENDIX 1

CHECKLIST—ACHIEVING COMMITMENT

A vital factor in increasing efficiency, productivity, competitiveness, and in maximising profits, is the commitment of people at all levels. Economic factors may have given people a greater understanding of the need for quality, customer service, and output, but when the economic winds blow again, there will need to be something more permanent if people are to give of their best at work.

There are fundamental difficulties in getting this commitment:

- size of the organisation
- advanced social situation where people no longer need to work to survive
- repetitive nature of most work
- high expectations
- increasing ineffectiveness of money alone to buy high performance in the mass of jobs.

One measure of our opportunities is to be seen in the days lost in absence. The Industrial Society specialises in the commonsense ways of gaining people's commitment. There is no one solution but there are a number of actions which must be taken to involve employees if maximum efficiency and profitability are to be obtained.

Effective leadership

1 Is there a published accountability chart which shows who is responsible for motivating whom? Are spans of control wide enough to encourage delegation and shorten the management chain, and small enough to motivate effectively—i.e. 4–15 people accountable to each boss at every level?
2 Is the status of the supervisor adequate to ensure that he or she can play an active part in the organisation at the first level of management?
3 Are all those people in charge of others on staff conditions?

Are their earnings more than the average of the top quarter of the people they supervise?

4 Is there a system of setting targets for every individual by their immediate leader, throughout the organisation?

5 Have all managers, including supervisors, received within the last three years instruction or re-instruction on the actions they need to take to get the best from their people?

6 Is there in existence a forum so that managers and supervisors can meet informally to discuss ways of improving performance?

7 Is there a management development plan? Is it being reviewed every two years?

8 Is there a known promotion procedure? Are vacant jobs advertised within the company?

Adequate communication

9 Is there a team briefing system whereby, at least once a month, the team leader at each level brings the whole of the team together to go over what is happening and why, in so far as it affects the group concerned?

10 Is the downward communication system reinforced by written material: e.g. newsletter?

11 Are noticeboards kept up-to-date? Is there an urgent section on the board where notices remain for only 48 hours?

12 Is there an upward mechanism of departmental consultative efficiency committees (unionised where unions are recognised)?

13 Is there an annual report to employees and an annual meeting of employees at each location where questions can be asked and answered?

14 Have steps been taken to prevent earnings fluctuating? Is there a system for recognising outstanding effort?

15 Is work study used to ensure performance levels are defined and standards maintained?

16 Are junior managers and supervisors involved in reviewing pay increases for those for whom they are responsible?

17 Are individuals told the reasons why pay increases have been granted, or why they have been withheld?

18 Is there a job evaluation scheme? Are there wage and salary structures?

19 Are steps being taken to reduce the counterproductive differences in status between manual and non-manual grades?

20 Are catering facilities, lavatories, and other physical conditions of work, up to the level of state-subsidised houses?

21 Are all other employee services reviewed at least every two years to ensure they aid high performance and are relevant to today's social situation?
22 Is there a redundancy policy? Will it function so as to help rather than hinder flexibility and job movement among employees to meet changes in conditions and technology?

Productive management–trade union policies

23 Where unions are recognised, has management clear policies to encourage the employees to join the union, attend its meetings, and to speak up for what they think is right?
24 Where unions are not recognised, does management have policies for achieving productive relationships at an early stage if unionism should start to grow?
25 Are there clear procedure agreements on grievance and negotiation for dealing with conflict?
26 Are union representatives seen by management on appointment and provided with letters of recognition? Do they receive any training to enable them to perform their role effectively?
27 Does management periodically talk to full-time trade union officials about matters affecting the business and its progress, rather than regard the official's sole function as appearing only at times of trouble?
28 Is there an effective procedure in existence for putting over a jointly-agreed announcement through union representatives and supervisors of the results of negotiations?

APPENDIX 2

ACTION-CENTRED LEADERSHIP

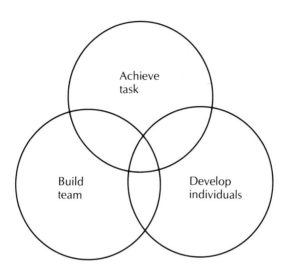

Key Actions		Task	Team	Individual
Define Objectives		Identify tasks & constraints	Hold team meetings Share commitment	Clarify objectives Gain acceptance
Plan	Gather Information	Consider options Check resources	Consult Encourage ideas Develop suggestions Assess skills	
	Decide	Priorities Time scales Standards	Structure	Allocate jobs Delegate Set targets
Brief		Clarify objectives Describe plan	Explain decisions Listen Answer questions Enthuse Check understanding	
Monitor Support		Assess progress Maintain Standards	Co-ordinate Reconcile conflict Recognise effort	Advise/praise Assist/reassure Counsel discipline
Evaluate		Summarise Review objectives Replan if necessary	Recognise & gain from success Learn from mistakes	Appraise performance
			Guide & train Give praise	

APPENDIX 3

CHECKLIST—POINTS FOR LEADERSHIP ACTION

1 Set the task of the team; put it across with enthusiasm and remind people of it often.
2 Instruct all leaders in the three circles; make them accountable for teams of 4–15.
3 Plan the work, check its progress, and design jobs or arrange work to encourage the commitment of individuals and the team.
4 Set individual targets after consulting; coach each person to achieve progress, at least once a year.
5 Delegate decisions to individuals; consult those affected.
6 Communicate the importance of each person's job; support and explain decisions to help people apply them; brief team monthly on Progress, Policy, People and Points for Action.
7 Train and develop people, especially those under 25; gain support for the rules and procedures, set an example and 'have a go' at those who break them.
8 Where unions are recognised, encourage joining, attendance at meetings, standing for office, and speaking up for what each person believes is in the interests of the organisation and all who work in it.
9 Serve people in the team and care for their wellbeing, improve working conditions and safety, work alongside people, deal with grievances promptly, and attend social functions.
10 Monitor action; learn from successes and mistakes; regularly walk round each person's place of work, observe, listen and praise.

FURTHER READING

Published by The Industrial Society:

The manager as a leader
The manager's guide to the behavioural sciences
The manager's responsibility for communication
Delegation
Effective discipline
Target setting
Appraisal and appraisal interviewing
Decision-taking
Preparing for the top
The work challenge

Also:

Basil, D.C. *Leadership skills for executive action*, New York: AMA

Drucker, P.F. *The practice of management*, London: Heinemann

Herzberg, F. *Work and the nature of man*, New York: World Publishing

McGregor, D. *The human side of enterprise*, New York: McGraw-Hill